Life is NC

We Thought...

My Biography

> Sometimes the Questions are complicated and the answers are simple.

Debbie E Forrest H

TreeHouse Publishers

www.gotreehouse.org

Printed in the United States of America

Copyright © 2022 Debbie E Forrest H

All rights reserved.

ISBN: 9798810088196

DEDICATION

<u>John 8:44</u>   Ye are of your father the devil, and the lusts of your father ye will do. He was a murderer from the beginning, and abode not in the truth, because there is no truth in him. When he speaketh a lie, he speaketh of his own: for he is a liar, and the father of it.

<u>Psalms 84:10</u> 10 For a day in thy courts is better than a thousand. I had rather be a doorkeeper in the house of my God, than to dwell in the tents of wickedness.

<u>Psalms 23:6</u> 6 Surely goodness and mercy shall follow me all the days of my life and I will dwell in the house of the Lord forever.

<u>Revelation 22:20</u> 20 He which testifieth these things saith, Surely, I come quickly. Amen. Even so, come, Lord Jesus.

All rights reserved. No part of this book may be copied or reproduced in any form, whether electronic, mechanical, photocopying, recordings, and otherwise without written permission from the author or publisher. Scripture references are from the *King James Version* of the Bible

~My biography, Proverbs 16 my Creator/Savior guides, Debbie E Forrest H~

This is Book #1 in the **"To Know Him" Series** with scriptural insight from *Isaiah 43:11 and John 17:3.*

Bible is used as foundation for this biography; the OT points to the fulfillment, as explained in the NT.

Dedications & Acknowledgements

My lifetime experience, plus studying - my favorite activity ☺

Dedicated to each person during my entire life:

- ❖ **To God** – My Creator and Redeemer (*Isaiah 40,43,53; I Timothy 3:16*). He supervised my conception and supervised my life, *Psalms 139*☺ bringing me all steps in my life (*Proverbs 16, Romans 8:28*) and to His Good & His Honor; in spite of my own lack & limitations

- ❖ **To my Dad** -Herman, who blessed me in spite of my errors

- ❖ **To my Mom** – Margaret, a role model who from very young 'outstood', 'inspired' in many areas in spite of lack of family origin support

- ❖ **To my Three Brothers and Theirs** - Richard, John & Bill

- ❖ **To my Husband** –Through Manuel, I was able to spend 45 years of my life in another culture; plus had the honor of becoming a mom to our three wonderful children; Deborah Margarita, Manuel III, and Joseph Manuel ☺

- ❖ **To Deb-Manuel-Joseph with Theirs -Corey, Angelica Grace, Patricia, and Sarah -** Thank you for caringly overlooking my faults - all going forth in life with good outlooks in spite of faults from their dads & moms, many knowing Jesus as Savior, plus willing to know Him better: each full of creative energy, clever, word-specialists, working with their partners in life with workable attitudes, overcomers, as Jesus/God our Creator is ☺

- ❖ **To my granddaughter Angelica Grace**- You beam when I simply listen to you. You are named after my grandmother (my mother's mother), Grace, and also after our children's nanny, Angelica Paz from that other culture who sewed, cooked, cleaned, gardened, and blessed us fully☺

- ❖ **To all family members** -grandparents, uncles, aunts, cousins in Texas, Colorado, Arkansas, California, Virginia and in my '45 year' country

- ❖ **To friends, including high school friends, and many other culture friends**, from different nations gained during my 45 years out of the USA, mentor friends especially and also those in the faith through Jesus, the Creator and Savior. **Included:** GC church & camps, English Bible studies, Sierra family, Pineda family, Whitsell mentor, Centro Conquista legal direction & counseling with Funes and Chang, GC church group with Andino family

- ❖ **To all those who share a great variety of key topics** through social media, like Dr. June Dawn Knight

Preface & Understanding

Genesis 3, humans ignoring our Genesis 1:28 assignment, from the beginning thus allows devil to dominate

I John 3:8, Ephesians 4:17-32, John 8:44, Colossians 3, James 3

Hosea 4:6 My people are destroyed for lack of knowledge……BECAUSE they rejected knowledge

He Who made ALL is ALL-Wise & True Love, John 15:13, Jeremiah 9:23-24, I Corinthians 1-2

The following *Jeremiah* verse was given to me by our Faithful God many years ago. He put His moon as testimony of Himself (*Psalms 89:36-37*): *Jeremiah 32:39-40:*

> *I will give you (Deb) one heart, one way, that you may fear Me forever, for your good and your children and theirs after them. I will make an everlasting covenant with them to do good towards them, putting My Fear in their hearts, so that they shall not depart from Me.*

Why do people *not* believe in the Creator of the creation? *Romans 1:17*-The righteousness of God revealed from *faith to faith*: the just shall live by faith (*Hebrews 11*).

The wrath of God is revealed from heaven against unrighteousness *that is held in Truth* because **that known of God is <u>manifest in us</u>.** He shows it to us: the invisible things of Him since the creation of the world ARE CLEARLY SEEN, through that made, His Eternal Power, *so that we are without excuse.*

We knew God, but glorified Him *not* as God, *neither* were thankful towards Him, but instead became vain in our imaginations and our foolish hearts was darkened, professing ourselves to be wise, we became foolish.☹ Unable to discern, *Hebrews 5:14,* we have mindlessly believed all or most of what we have been taught in the worldly systems: education of all levels, commercials, videos, 'experts', etc. And lastly, we do not dig for true wisdom and true understanding, Proverbs 2 & 8.☹ Pharisees taught ideas; Jesus taught how to use heart wisely to heal and be healed, to bless and be blessed, but truly **"believing" in Him and through Him, is a life-time battle** that is worth eternity with our wonderful God/Creator/Savior, *II Corinthians 13:5.*

From Adam until Jesus crucified are 4000 years, calculated carefully using the Old Testament (OT). We are close to 2000 years since He arose. Why is this key? The Millennium would then make 7000 years likened unto seven days of creation affirmed in *Exodus 20:11*. The building of the Tower of Babel was stopped because God-Creator-Redeemer KNEW that we humans would not stop until becoming as "gods".

This is the lie that Satan told Eve. In addition, our imaginations can be limitless, *Genesis 6:5*.

Our now-a-day tower is the DIGITAL world with artificial intelligence (AI) system built by us. Why? God knowing us from before conception (*Jeremiah 1:5, Psalms 139*), leaves us free to choose, even foolishly, yet does aid us because He is Love as shown through Jesus, *Romans 5*. ☺

He does all of this without digital, giving us 'choice', but Satan (his adversary) needs internet/digital/AI to "know" us by our data & thereby control us. This is coming up fast.☹

What does this mean? We are made in God's Image, *Genesis 1*. Each person is made special by Him, *Psalms 139*, with unique fingerprints, personality, and abilities. We are made new through His Blood (*John 1:12-13, II Corinthians 5, Hebrews 10:19*) through our faith in Him, *Ephesians 2*. During this temporary life while in our physical body, each with our own inner soul, unlike animals, we face tremendous challenges, especially relational, *Romans 8:20-22, Ecclesiastes, and Job*.

We are called to **wisely** choose God and God-Level limits so to live righteously blessing ourselves, *Proverbs 4:23*, honoring Him as our Creator/Savior with these 'good' fruits, *Ephesians 2:10*, so our fellow humans can be blessed towards His Eternal realm. ☺

The 'Metaverse' through artificial intelligence (AI) augmented 'reality' as designed by non-perfect humans, is an imaginary disembodied limitless world, that can leave our bodies exposed spiritually, *Ephesians 6:12*.

There, virtual properties can be bought and sold; humans can participate as virtual god-like self-images changing as is pleasing to self. There, each can experience limitless freedom space-wise, timewise, identity-wise, addicting-wise, no longer facing reality relational-wise, not able to love God directly nor neighbors as in real life.

The ISSUE is that we Do die physically, but our inner souls cannot be uploaded into a computer and our thoughts are only fully known by God Himself, *Matthew 9:4, 12:25; Luke 5:22*. Our thoughts can only be 'predicted' by this AI algorithm system through data collected about us in our daily lives. Full Deceit is this realm because it detracts from reality here and later in eternity. At present in 2022, AI is being encouraged to be used in businesses instead of traditional ways, which means that instead of analyzing business earnings through traditional ways, AI will use the huge amount of personal data of customers, resulting in probability-driven data, to have faster larger earnings, so the love to have more is non-stop which easily excludes the necessary key development of other more important living aspects of this temporary life.

Any genome data taken from creation design itself will be ever-increasing as it is God-size massive data just as social data can be as we are creatures of preferences, constantly changing. My young granddaughter already talks about her 'changing' friends through an imaginary button on her arm.

It is desired that the human-developed AI probability-system will govern we humans because it is being fed our data and it is given programmable ways to 'create' their very own ways or programs, with the 'ambition' installed to rule. The source of this is from human non-perfect thinking. ☹ Add to this, the Agenda 2030 with the World Economic Forum who have stated now in 2022 that they are systematically dwindling food supplies in different ways to cause the supposedly bettered socialistic world RESET with a digital money, using the excuse of the "climate" agenda to reduce carbon which we are made of and breathe, as plants too, therefore air chemicalized purifiers will reduce carbon through chemicals in buildings, airplanes, businesses.

In other words, forests are being cut down commercially world-wide, including destructive mining practices reducing normal climate cycles plus climate engineering occurs. Finally, education worldwide is an indoctrination system for this agenda away from our God's wisdom and original creation.

Our knowledge of our Creator and His Wisdom is low key ☹ So He did the 'simple' way for us, that He Himself came to solve this for us, *I Timothy 3:16, II Corinthians 11:3, II Corinthians 11:3.* ☺

Conclusion: John Piper gives in his book "When We don't desire God, how to fight for joy in Him", *Deuteronomy 28:47-48* 'Because you serve NOT your God-Creator-Redeemer with joyfulness and gladness of heart for the abundance of all things, therefore shall you serve your enemies (our own mind in vainness is our worst enemy, *Ecclesiastes*).

God wants us to be very glad in Him, *Romans 1:21, Philippians 4:4.* Piper continues saying that the devil knows all trueness about God, yet God is not honored by him because Satan wants to be god above the One True God and tries to reach his goal through ungodly ways, *John 8:44.* Finally, Piper concludes that when we come to treasure God/Creator/Savior (parable, finding best pearl and selling all to have it), desire Him, know Him, and delight in Him Who is All Wise and pursues us ☺ thereby we will be a blessing to people even enemies, just as He gave Himself for us when enemies, *Romans 5*. THEN He is truly honored ☺

> Today you are YOU,
> that is TRUER than true.
> There is NO ONE alive
> who is YOUER than YOU!
> ~Dr. Suess

With Love, Debbie E. Forrest H.

God gave you a fingerprint that no one else has

So you can leave an imprint that no one else can.

CONTENTS

Dedication & Acknowledgments

Preface & Understanding

01	My Legacy	Pg	01
02	Born, Raised, Jesus, Wedding	Pg	03
03	Married, Salvation from Self	Pg	07
04	Family & Master's Degree	Pg	13
05	Insights After my Master's Degree	Pg	21
06	COVID, Return to USA	Pg	41

Appendices:

A	**Who is Jesus?**	Pg	49
B	**Timeline**	Pg	53
C	**True Astronomy**	Pg	57

Key phrases: not like non-mathematical life, Jesus, "married' to settle, another country to not follow status quo, becoming a mom, great commission church to share about Jesus, 'seeing' how our God-Creator-Redeemer Wisely oversees, natural/homeopathic health, "abuse' versus standing up for self, master's degree to 'discern' deep lies & real truths, return to USA blessing my family and gaining Piper's teaching to enjoy our God, my loving outdoor cat.☺

Isaiah 43:11 **'I, even I, am God and beside Me there is no savior'.**

1
My Legacy

- ✧ Bless, You, dear God-Creator-Redeemer, O my soul and all that is within me; bless Your Holy Name. Bless You, forgetting not all Your benefits: Who forgives all my iniquities and who heals all my diseases ☺ Who redeems my life from destruction! Who crowns me with Your Loving-Kindness, Your Tender Mercies. *Psalms 103:1-4*

- ✧ I waited patiently for my God/Creator; He inclined unto me, heard my cry. He brought me up out of my own-made horrible pit, out of my own miry clay, and set my feet upon A Rock (Jesus) establishing my goings.

    He has put a new song in my mouth, praise unto my God.

    Many shall see it, and fear Him correctly, and trust Him. *Psalms 40:1-3*

- I will lift up my eyes unto the hills, from whence comes my help. My help comes from God/Creator, who made heaven and earth. *Psalms 121:1-2*

- Giving thanks unto the Father, who has made us to be partakers of the inheritance of the saints in Light (*John 1*) Who has delivered us from the power of darkness and translated us into the kingdom of His dear Son, His only begotten Son, In whom we have redemption through His Blood, even the forgiveness of our sins. Who is The Image of The Invisible God/Creator (*Romans 1*)?For by Him (Jesus) were all things created, that are in heaven and in earth, visible and invisible, thrones, dominions, principalities, powers: all things were created by Him, and for Him: And He is before all things, and by Him all things exist. He is the Head of the body, the church. *Colossians 1:13-18*

2

Born, Raised, Jesus, Wedding

I was born in Tyler Texas, USA. I lived in different Texas cities while my brothers were being born in Austin, Waco, and finally Temple. About the time of Kennedy-Nixon election, my life began to take a turn for the worse. With people relations, I began to be disgruntled about life. None of that was according to my math-step thinking, ha-ha, but I admit that I did not suffer terribly in other ways as some children do.

I began my very young non-social approach which lasted through 9th grade. In the tenth grade, I was feeling better, with two years of chemistry classes plus *Slide Rule* club and volleyball. I graduated from Temple High School in 1971 having lived during the 'Beatle' music period, dancing to *Hey Jude*, internally believing that a guy could be my solution to happiness. Yet through Vacation Bible School 1965 at First Baptist Church, a most important event occurred of me receiving Jesus as my Savior at 12 years old. I remember my 'refreshing' baptism in Him.☺ A great memory.☺

Yet as a typical churchgoer, without mentorship as Jesus indicates in Matthew 28 under His own authority, I proceeded to live according to the times of the moment, light sexual perversion, yet no drugs nor smoke nor drink.

Our consent to anything lesser than God's laws and/or God's wisdom, gives the enemy rights over us.

> *Psalms 14:14 - The fool hath said in his heart, There is no God. They are corrupt, they have done abominable works, there is none that doeth good.*

Thereby in this ignorance plus my own temporary life desires, my descendants were affected; yet His Hand has aided us. ☺

In the university at Nacogdoches Texas where we moved, my technical drawing class was in the forestry building. Four men studying forestry were in that class, from the country where I lived for 45 years. I met others from that country that were studying forestry here. Then, I met the one whom I married. I visited that country, after we dated, and he proceeded to show me all about it.

I finished my three major degrees in mathematics, physics, and chemistry in Texas, then married and went to that country in 1975. I felt like his country matched my personality, very natural. It was refreshing and I liked it tremendously.

My mother enjoyed coming to visit us on many occasions as well as my grandmother, especially when each of our children were born. Also, my dad visited us as well as my brothers, aunts, and cousins, each once or twice. We toured all of the west part of the country with them ☺

Gleaning and scanning, combined with strategies to memorize is how I achieved very good grades, yet not the best. To this day, I still do this but truly this is a limiting factor in that I do not gain into my soul a depth of information necessary to be able to teach well, plus am not spontaneous, so teaching is an extremely difficult activity for me. But I can emit brief concise written ideas based on gathering many puzzle pieces, which provides a gleaned output.☺

Up to this point, my life was good; I felt good. Yet as most women, I desired to marry but with no clue about "how to be married". And furthermore, it seems that marriage draws out things hidden in our hearts from infancy. Quite challenging indeed! Who would have known?

He, who became my husband, had graduated in 1972, returned home to his country and then returned to Texas in 1974 for a six-month scholarship, so we married.

Our wedding in December 1974 was at my family's home in our living room, which had beautiful red velvet wallpaper, with red shaggy carpet and white arcs towards the lowered level with its fireplace. It was beautiful. Plus, my mom (Margaret) made my dress ☺ She and my grandmom (her mom, Grace) cooked the foods offered, as the wedding occurred at noon.

The pastor who married us was from that same country as my husband, but he was living with his American bride in the USA. My husband's sister flew in, and my cousins came plus my brothers, grandparents and others. Very nice home wedding, car painted adequately ha-ha, then a road trip to deliver his sister to an airport. We returned for Christmas to be with my family then continued our travels in USA, until travelling by car to our destined country where I lived 45 years until God Almighty convinced me wisely to stay in the USA during the special 2020 'COVID' year.

So, then the 'married' season began…

3

Married, Salvation From Self

There, living in that country, married, God Almighty could then 'take me through the wildernesses to see what was in my heart, *Deuteronomy 8:2*. It revealed several ungodly heart roots from childhood throughout my years there. It definitely caused me to know Him much better, *Jeremiah 9:24*. I remember while in university, considering Him to some degree and being involved in "Christian" activities. Recently there in that country, a traditional Christian pastor aided me briefly about who the Jews are. Then another church aided us all, meaning our three children to receive Jesus as their Savior; plus, we learned how to share about Jesus to others so they could 'receive Him' also, *John 1:12-13*.

Missing in most churches worldwide is depth teaching: the old covenant is the shadow, as described in *Hebrews*, giving way to Jesus as God/Creator and Savior, Who fulfilled all to freely give us His Righteousness, *I Timothy 3:16, II Corinthians 5:19*.

Also, the fact that the churches do not explain that God Himself seals our deal by bearing us NEW through His Holy Spirit (*II Corinthians 13:5* make sure you truly have faith in Him, *II Corinthians 5, Ephesians 1:13-14, John 3*).

My first year there, at almost 23 years old, I taught physics and chemistry to 11th and 12th grades at a bilingual high school. Those students were only a few years younger than I.

I changed jobs to work in a Meat Exportation Quality Control lab, then worked in a mining-petroleum government lab during which time our daughter was born. She was born with white skin and dark hair - a joy to people when we were in USA, as they used to blond-haired babies during that particular time.

She was always modeling, chatty, caring for her brothers and at 12 she became artistic. She also translated when her grandmom visited. My daughter is named after me, and her second name is after my mother, Margarita.

When I was pregnant with our first son, I began a new job traveling, selling industrial water treatments for boilers and water towers, which I did until we opted for homeschooling. This son, named after his dad, was a busy climbing child - yet kind one.

He had many active ideas which resulted in frequent bumps on his head and as second children go, fewer pictures taken of him ☹

My favorite pictures of each were the loss of their first tooth, pictures I have in my bedroom presently.☺

Our three children were born in that country, where to my total agreement, we opted for homeschooling offering a certain protection from early-on common place perversions that can occur anywhere in this post-modern world.

During that time period, I, who had been operated on to not have more children at the young age of 28, had a tiny conversation with God about that in 1985. He literally worked out the details so that my same gynecologist in that country, re-operated me to have another child in 1986. This talented son, a blessing to his siblings, named after Joseph, second to Pharaoh as a good manager which this son is, was also named after his dad.

Meanwhile we met the Sierra family going to that church. They taught us about sharing Jesus with others (see Appendix A Who is Jesus?), also introducing us to homeschooling. As a consequence, we attended that church plus its camps at Easter time; all very informative about our salvation, yet not in depth through the Bible.

Home-schooling was introduced to us through the Sierra family as well, offering ACE material that they used with their six children. Schools were setup with this system in several countries due to their influence.

It is a simple basics-learning material with character forming ideas, only requiring study for a few hours per day. Our children completed through 12th grade at home and had no problem functioning in university settings. More challenging than the educational setup, as for most churchgoers, is coming to truly taking steps to function in God and God's Wisdom, believing Him and in Him, as we go, *Jeremiah 2:13*.

The world has a multitude of man-engineered religions, but the older biblical covenants with the new testament requiring a testator, shows God's Wisdom, *I Corinthians 1-2*, with the creation as basis of proof.

Jesus' own teachings explained that keeping God's Laws is indeed a heart matter, plus He healed because His Goal is our entire soul-body wholeness in connection with Himself, as our Creator and Savior. The miracles that He did were the most exceptional in history, as the Bible covers such. So, we can see why Nicodemus in *John 3* said that Jesus had to have come from God as evidenced by so many special works or miracles.

The law guides us to Him who is righteous, but through Him, we live!

The Pineda family was sent by this church to Venezuela, and I visited them, there being introduced to homeopathic medicine through church members, when at that same time period, certain "normal western" medicines were damaging me, not curing. Since that time, I have used a more natural approach as my own true health care, using herbs and similar as needed, not often, plus with the use of eating principals given in *Daniel 1* and *Daniel 10* to gain health. Hard to do! Definitely God has designed our bodies to go towards health, but we ingest much that does not allow that process to maximize itself. Hard subject to deal with, indeed! We could also trust Him for our health ☺

In 2017, my white blood count was too low plus I had several non-healthy symptoms, so I chose for seven days to only eat vegetables, fruits, rice and beans, *Daniel 1*. It would have been advantageous to do it longer, but we hate to not eat.☹ Anyway, I was cured and good for months. ☺ My health experience with foods, once living again in USA, 2020 on, convinced me to not eat out much and to avoid most processed foods. We at present, have lost the understanding of plants and trees for health, as designed by God.

Instead, we give our newborns, artificial milks ☹ so they are constipated at a tiny age. ☹

In a similar time period, I had a failed pregnancy at 42, during which time through visitors, my dear God who watches over us, *Psalms 139,* gave me…

> *Psalms 46:10 Be still and know that I am God; I will be exalted among the heathen, I will be exalted in the earth.*

I thought to myself, "Wow I need to do this, recognize that HE IS GOD!" This verse began for me an upward climb in Jesus ☺ and this reminds me of ….

> *Romans 5:3-5 And not only so, but we glory in tribulations also: knowing that tribulation works patience, and patience, experience and experience, hope, and hope makes not ashamed because the love of God is shed abroad in our hearts by the Holy Ghost which is given unto us.*

4

Family & Master's Degree

Forrest, being my maiden name, I married a forester, and our first son was born on Arbor Day in that country, plus he was born on the birthday of his dad's brother, Jose Manuel who perished at 13. And furthermore, our youngest son has exactly that same name but in English. Our daughter was born on Christmas Day in that country, the 24th of December close to my birthday which I had desired months before.☺

Life is NOT full of random unique coincidences but is accomplished by *Romans 8:28* and *Psalms 139*, where our Author and Finisher of our Salvation is the COORDINATOR above ALL Coordinators through **His** Wisdom, *Proverbs, Romans 5, I Corinthians 1-2*, so that **the most will be saved** towards Himself, through promises made to Abraham, *Isaiah 44:6, I Corinthians 1:26-31, 2:8, Romans 11* all grafted into Israel, *Revelation 7:9*.

In 1993, Father God, *Genesis 1:1, John 1 Jesus, John 17:3*, began showing me 'to see' WHAT HE DOES AROUND US as He brings things to His Level of Good, *Romans 8:28*, just as we are saved by His Righteousness and Blood, not by any of our own "good".

He blesses each person in many different ways, but we usually do not 'see this'. Jesus washed Judas' feet and then called Judas, 'friend', at the moment of giving Jesus the fatal kiss.

> ***Romans 5, For if, when we were enemies, we were reconciled to God by the death of his Son, much more, being reconciled, we shall be saved by his life.***

I add to this "seeing God at work" analysis, that each of my children, in what I call "least probable circumstances", met their spouses. Our guys have 'rolled' with their women, meaning a type of leadership that gives space to each to grow inwards and actively, while our God/Creator aids us. ☺

BACK TO MY MARRIAGE

The marriage did not develop well due to lack of character of both and the devil surely aided, plus churches in general ignore how to aid and advise.

So, prior to our collapse in 2014, God, ahead of the game, impressed on me in 2011, that I did not remember much about second grade.

Then in 2012, a missionary Whitsell called me and a couple of others to participate in several teaching sessions given by her about inner-heart healing or freeing of heart entanglements developed by us when we are young as we faced different difficult situations that we did not like. All used the *Elijah House Prayer Ministry* teachings and methods. Wow was that key for me because I discovered that way back in second grade, I already disliked the normal usual family striving dynamics, plus my dad begun to be gone lots to earn more money, so I blocked myself from 'social' including in family to a huge degree and as a consequence, became socially fearful and socially awkward.

By having a beginning of being freed, when the surprising marriage collapse occurred in 2014, although I sought much advice through lawyers and pastors, yet finding no solution, I was able to receive instruction and direction from some of Whitsell's friends who were specialists in these kinds of situations. I was sure to seize on this God-given opportunity as I got to know them.

This lawyer-pastor Funes and his aid Chang have a ministry called *Centro Conquista*, based in that country, both from that country. They teach about abuse, which in a "church world", I had never heard about that before nor have most churchgoers.

They aided me with legal actions and advice, constantly teaching me about what abuse looks like, offering me protection 24/7 which was very welcome. I was more than pleased to be taught because of two major disrespectful things that had occurred around that same time, this as a result of growing abuse with no strategies to stop it.

All three of them covered me emotionally, plus gave me valuable insights during those times so that I could learn to stand up for myself. I did learn through their teachings during several years' time. I am very grateful to them!

During that time period, God Almighty blessed me in many other details that I will never forget. God the Father was right on time with help, when I saw no answer and He Himself blessed my life events to unfold which included husband no longer in our house by his very own doings, a nephew coming to rent in my home while my youngest son moved to the USA.

Before that, my son and I cried together twice over our family losses. Later my nephew's sister and later a friend of theirs also rented so I had company plus income.☺

Plants in my yard blessed me more than normal like a rose plant that gave me ten roses repeatedly and several bougainvillea that flowered purple 100% when never before!☺

And friends too blessed me on special occasions; meanwhile all our adult children were living in the USA.

The same friend Whitsell proceeded to take me to a special missionary camp close by where we lived. I had the privilege of meeting many missionaries in that country who bless people in great variety of ways. An added pleasant blessing is that my husband has covered me financially during these years. Perhaps we are not yet "officially divorced" because the only religious advice was 'do not divorce', yet Funes and Chang taught me that a marriage is not about 'official, legal' but about a relational development as such.

Theology at our Great Commission church aided us to know God better plus their Easter camps caused me to gain understanding about *Romans 1*, that by His Creation, He is known.

And thereby, I learned eventually to ENJOY HIM through enjoying His CREATION.☺

And furthermore, I learned to be thankful as *Roman 1* states, instead of thinking myself wise WITHOUT HIM thereby continuing in foolishness; this has taken an entire lifetime ☺

Our marriage by this time was getting very non-functional but I, as a very naïve person, did not realize the depth of that. God Almighty grew me in emotional maturity and understanding during my lifetime.

So in about 2015, I was good to go in this part. However, in 2020-2022 I was challenged yet again by living newly in the USA. My innermost heart has come to follow Him lots better now. ☺

That year 2015, I cared for my mom, and saw clearly that I needed to mature emotionally even more and am sure that God the Father showed me just that. ☺.

At the COVID time, I find myself ousted from where I had lived for almost 45 years. My children already having made their lives in the USA, did not want me to risk travelling by air. This change plus the 'times' we live in, have challenged me to go from a passive simple older life to a more active heart life in Jesus, having a bettered God-purpose life to serve my adult children and theirs, especially my daughter and her daughter. ☺.

My Master's Degree

My astrophysics master's degree, an idea that I did not have on my mind to accomplish, suddenly was available in 2008 in that same country in the National University where we lived. I thought, "for fun, I will do it". Turns out that…

(1) It was all in Spanish and I had never studied in Spanish before, so a plus.

(2) I had to rapidly authenticate my University USA bachelor's degree from 1974, which was not unreasonably difficult, because I had **obtained a triple major degree.**

(3) They did not use much math as compared to a USA degree, which allowed me to study 10 hours a day as it was in Spanish.

(4) When I did presentations, I could hear that my speaking ability in Spanish must be improved, so I practiced my presentations, and I was not familiar with scientific terms in Spanish. I definitely enjoyed it. We even made a telescope out of ordinary objects, my four fellow classmates aiding in detail.

Finishing classes in 2012, I graduated in 2016.

I was pleased to complete the degree with honors, but little did I know, that as the natural health knowledge given to me was key to my bettered way of thinking, this knowledge would aid me in the new challenging of mainstream ideas that I would be exposed to during the next few years - facts and observations that proved that many 'so called truths' were different from much of what we were taught in our education. On many occasions, simple experiments that I myself and others would do and still do, have proven differences. Some say that this the true way to do science ☺

Conclusion on this part, our Eternal God/Creator/Savior, *Isaiah 43:11*, *Psalms 139*, *Romans 8:28* spectacularly works on our lives ☺ wahoo ☺.

5

Insights after my Master's Degree

I suspect that the "Pinky's who wanna rule this world" observe that we 'normal' citizens, literally believe all we are taught in schools worldwide, for decades. So recently like in 2015 or so, 'they' began to put out 'truths' that have caused many to reevaluate and test in an attempt to understand real truths about where we live, but their purposes include keeping us busy and divided among ourselves, while they bring us to a new world governance through a challenging route - as the World Economic Forum in 2022 openly stated this year.

They are systematically changing our normal food chain, and times will become difficult while the World RESET continues. We have been recently given the *Rockefeller Lockstep Program.*[1]

---
[1] https://www.rockefellerfoundation.org/blog/innovating-for-a-bold-future/

We know about Agendas 21 & 2030 'sustainability plan' plus the Silent War document explains how we are mathematically being tested over and over so they can gain social data for their models that will rule the Earth. While my biography greatly informs you of the MAGNIFICIENCE of our God-Creator-Savior in my life and my children's (*Hebrews 11* lives by faith, Charles Swindoll's biographies and more), it also informs you of this particular time in the history of almost 6000 years since creation and its implications (see Appendix B Timeline).

If you desire to know and understand, it is only worthwhile being accompanied by a growing true knowing of our Creator through whom we exist, being 'saved' only through His Son by His Righteousness. Then we go forward better in this life and into Eternity with Him.

I will be discussing in this chapter some of these following ideas that have come about in recent times. Noel put this list out to the public, and as I am very nerdy plus my master's degree has permitted me to "see" into many of the following ideas, I share this:

Written around 2017, by Noel Joshua Hadley:[2]

After learning about the fake moon landings, the Federal Reserve, chemtrails, fluoride, vaccines, chip implants, 5g, warring bloodlines, 9/11 and any number of false flag attacks or hoaxes like the Gulf of Tonkin, crisis actors who keep showing up at different psycho-dramatic exercises intended to social engineer us into MkUltra zombies, the CIA's hand in music and television and sexuality and women's rights and family life and practically everything, how space is fake, the earth is not a globe, Antarctica is the edge of the earth and the firmament is a solid dome above us, stars are identified with living beings, the germ theory is a lie, evolution is a lie, giants and probably mythological beings are real, the gods war over us like chess pieces, Scientism and the Occult are happily wed, the Mysteries surround us, real history is buried and fake history is written as a textbook reality, they lied about the Bolshevik Revolution, they lied about the fact that the United States is in actuality a corporation and money isn't even real and Abraham Lincoln actually sold us all into slavery to the state, how the Georgia Guidestones and the United Nations want us all dead and are actively going about to make it happen, pedophilia and Satanic ritual abuse are everywhere, entertainment and politics alike are as scripted as a media teleprompter and the world is one big stage and Zionism and Freemasonry and the Roman Catholic Church and the Jesuits and Illuminati and other secret societies like Skull & Bones rule the world, and most importantly of all, it's all ultimately run and managed from the top by Satan, prince of power of the air and the father of lies—and after rightly concluding how the kings and the sovereigns of the earth are conspiring against Yahuwah, the Most-High, and want Him dead, some of you simply need more Trump.

---

[2] https://theunexpectedcosmology.com/the-watchers-have-been-released-from-prison-and-theyre-here-to-deceive-us/

More: 9/11 dynamite which I heard about in early 2000's on my dad's tv, Sandy Hook destroyed, Boston Massacre with pressure cooker, Vatican-Muslim connection, dew fires in California and Australia not burning trees around, pre-rapture history, and humanism.

Since staying in USA, in 2020, I have followed a White House Correspondent for WATB.tv, Dr. June Dawn Knight, who reported during Trump's administration and concluded after a time there, that no leader is truly 'for' us but instead follows 'agendas. Learn more about her at www.watb.tv.

Do not be deceived: *Matthew 24:5* states that Jesus answered them, Take heed that no man deceives you for many shall come in My Name (*Philippians 2:9*), saying 'I am Christ', deceiving many. *11* Many false prophets shall rise and deceive many (*verse 16* abomination desolation begins last 42 months, *Daniel 9:27, Revelation 13*).

23 if any man says to you, 'Lo, here is Christ, or there', believe it not, for there shall arise false Christs and false prophets, showing great signs and wonders insomuch that, if it were possible, they could deceive the very elect (whose names written in the book of life of the slain Lamb, plan since Foundation of this world, *Revelation 13:8*).

Behold, I have told you **before that** if they shall say to you, 'Behold, He is in the desert, go not forth. Behold, He is in the secret chambers; believe it not. For as the lightning comes out of the east and shines to the west, so shall also the coming of the Son of Man be. For wheresoever the carcass is, there will the eagles be gathered together (*Luke 17:36-37, Revelation 19:17-19*).

II Thessalonians.2:1-4 We beseech you, brethren, by the coming of our Jesus Christ **and** by our gathering together **to** Him (*I Thessalonians 4:15-17*) that you are not soon shaken in mind or be troubled, neither by spirit nor by word nor by letter as from us, for the day of Jesus Christ is at hand. **Let no man deceive you by any means** for that day shall not come, except there comes a falling away **first** (denying that Jesus is **THE** Savior) **and** the man of sin **be revealed**, the son of perdition who opposes the True God Creator and tries to exalt himself above all that is called 'God' or that is worshipped.

Atheists talk about "god' constantly yet *Psalms 14* 'A fool said in his heart, 'there is no God'**.**

'Expert' hoax: Sciences & Western medicine is presented in a business-like way, excluding our Creator and most information given through His Word.

Medical testing is the norm given by protocols as well as results and treatments, that usually are dissonant (not in unity with), yet no questions asked by patients. On the other hand, no true orientation is given to go home, do a ten-day *Daniel 1* vegetarian diet, and then retest. Specialists deal with special parts of our bodies, yet the body functions as a whole. Many plants and trees, like cinnamon bark, are healing substances provided by our Creator. An example: *II Chronicles 16:12* 'Asa in the thirty and ninth year of his reign was diseased in his feet, until his disease was exceeding great, yet in his disease he sought not to God Creator, but to the physicians. Diabetes, a most common issue, is in fact a metabolism issue in which glucose hooks up with hemoglobin, thereby reducing oxygen usage in the body. Probable solution: a vegetarian diet for 10 days ☺

His Creation, no small thing, which He established BY SPEAKING (*Psalms 33:6*) through Water that was already present.

It thereby produced light being the electromagnetic spectrum, made on first 24-hour day (*Exodus 20:11*), process called sonoluminescence.

The second day, He separated the water over the abysm to be the waters above and the waters below, making air/space in between called the Firmament of His Power, *Psalm 150:1*.

*D*istance not measurable (*Jeremiah 31:37*), yet not light-years as so-called science calculates based on an "assumed, measured" speed of light as the size of the sun is also. The parallax arc method calculates the Sun's distance yet when driving along, Sun rays can be observed at angles in about 1/3 of the circumference in that location, but the middle rays are VERTICAL because the Sun is truly close by and not large as has been calculated. The Sun is also called a star by science but not by God, *Genesis 1, I Corinthians 15*, (see Appendix C).

On the third day, He had the waters below gathered so that 'dry land could appear', then planted it and setup an underground sprinkling system, yet no rain yet (*Genesis 2:5-6*). For the fourth 24-hour day, it was then necessary for the plants, that the Sun and its resonant (life giving) light rays be given, resonant for us too, but not in excess.

The sun and the moon are both a light source, *Genesis 1*; unlike what science teaches us about moon reflecting the sun's light. The stars also are 'living' light sources (*Revelation 1:20*).

Each of these light sources have their own glory *(I Corinthians 15:40-41)*, all to give light, to divide night from day, to be for signs and seasons and days and years.

People have measured the temperature effect of the moonlight at night as cold in comparison with the Sun's, a different glory as stated in *I Corinthians 15*.

On day five, He made creatures in water and in air, which are innumerable *(Psalms 104:25)*.

Then on day six, He made land animals, yet we humans out of dust *(Genesis 2:7)* then breathed into our nostrils the breath of life, made in His image, NOT A SMALL THING. We are not as ANIMALS! I believe He had FUN creating as there is SO much variety, including the uniqueness of each human being; likewise, He gives unique insight to each person in very unique ways during their lifetime☺

The bible timeline is true history proven by archaeology versus history timelines and details and stories as given to us through education. Interventions by our God in what we call 'miracles' begins with His Creation itself and all its magnificent details.☺

- When the world flood came about, Noah and family were protected plus also the innumerable sea creatures and plants in the seas. Afterward, the trees budded understood by the dove that brought a branch with leaves to Noah.

- At Tower of Babel, God dispersed the descendants of Japheth, Shem, and Ham, stopping humanity from their vain thinking, *Jeremiah 2:13*, as we observe now in 2022.

- Angels supped with Abraham.

- Jacob wrestled with an angel.

- Moses saw God directing Aaron's rod to become a snake, water to blood, extra frogs, lice called the Finger of God, locusts directed towards them, flies but Goshen was protected.

- Terrible darkness when first born died but those with sacrificed lamb blood over their doors as God directed were protected.

- THE RED SEA opened WITH DRY land to pass over.

- In the desert wilderness 2 million people were fed by meat, water, manna (angel's food, *Psalms 78:25*) until they arrived at The Land where all was already built and cultivated. ☺

- Joshua held Moses' arms up so battle would be won, *Exodus 17:12-14.*

- Gideon, a farmer, called to be a warrior for our God, tested God in two ways to confirm - dew on cloth and next day, dew not on cloth.

- Elijah experienced ravens feeding him, fire from heaven, running faster than others.

- Elisha with double portion from God.

- As well as Daniel and his friends saved in burning furnace with Jesus there, from lions.

- Nicodemus testified about Jesus' workings that He must be from God, *John 21:25.*

So, this was Jesus' calling card as God on Earth, *I Timothy 3:16, II Corinthians 5:19.* This is some of what has been understood by me, by listening to many others, and studying the bible as God's Word.

Since my Graduation from my Astrophysics Master's Degree:

Education system excludes the Creator, as if we exist without Him and as if all came to exist without an intelligent being, as if original thoughts came from nowhere.

We at best can only manipulate aspects of His Creation. Example: moon is a light made by God, has its own light, *Genesis 1:14-18*.

More than not, we give our children (worldwide) over to government "education" and church-theories, without studying. Education could be given as practical *'Proverbially'* wise, common sense for relationships & other such skills (*James 3*), how to work (not just find a job), learning to create business opportunities, wise money and nutritional food management, value of each person according to Our Creator and much more.

Most **sciences** are based on many assumptions excluding knowledge of Creator, like astronomy that bases all on the statement that the sun is a star and it that suddenly ignites as such, millions of years later flinging planets off to orbit that 'sun', plus through more millions of years, simple life forms 'miraculously' begin little by little adding its necessary parts based on 'enough time and crystal-like non-living self-assembly' to become functional intricate 'living' beings.

Does anyone ask how a first atom with such power could have established itself without an intelligence being?

The basis for millions and billions of years comes in part from the slope equation of Hubble's graph on his 'galaxy' data in early 1900's, presupposing that light has a velocity which is half the distance to our sun.

Student debt and/or such loans for degrees make no financial sense; the same money invested in business does, *Proverbs 24:27*.

At present in 2022, traditional business methods are being discouraged while everyone is being 'pushed' towards gathering data (massive data amounts) to 'drive' that data to be the guide to better faster income, through **algorithm probability with artificial intelligence** computers. These are being programmed by humans so that these AI programs will 'develop their own programs', yet these machines are not aware as we, nor empathetic, therefore not responsible for consequences of programs they make and can easily be against 'we the people'.

Genomic data is much more massive because our Creator Wonderfully created. Will **Robots** be more perfect than humans? **They can hold 'memory' better than we but lack because** Humans beings have a soul & are made in THE Creator's image plus are saved through Him so we can worship and thank Him.

Robots do not have such a soul and are programmed through humans who have errors. If existing, 'aliens' are not 'saved' nor angels, as Jesus saves those made in His Image only.

Psychology is taught without basic wisdom and understanding of our Creator, so is at best an emotional, self-focus for self-interest and preferences. God who made us in His Image is Love yet Judges perfectly too AND gave His own self as fully Righteous to save any unrighteous humans who are willing to go towards Him in His Truth. He is our Example.

Furthermore, He designed each person while in the womb, *Psalms 139,* for His own God-Honor and for His Righteous Purposes, to bless human beings to come to Him *(OT, I Corinthians 1-2, Romans 11, Revelation 7:9).* **Lusts** (addictions) **and contention** are considered normal yet are deceitful as their fruit will not be appetizing in the long-run, *James 3.*

Biology uses 'evolution' and 'selection' ideas as if these were intelligent operations, but at best, those ideas refer to random activity through death processes, as opposed to *life* building processes where death exists by falling short of God and God's Wisdom, *Jeremiah 2:13.*

'Scientists' are on the lookout for a natural algorithm that explains the origin of all including 'life' excluding the Creator, as if we are only material but we DO have a soul, *I Corinthians 5:5.*

An algorithm is not an intelligent operator. Teresa Woodruff describes 'zinc spark' when the conception of an animal occurs, one incredible detail of THE CREATION, therein an abortion of an unborn human baby is a death penalty for that unborn, not even considered as a common procedure for unborn animals. Through the false evolution story, humans are mistakenly classified as animals, yet we are made in our Creator's image and saved by His Blood. ☺

Many **rocks are organic** anatomy parts mostly from pre-flood creatures of ALL sizes (*Genesis 6:4*), idea useful perhaps to deceive us through blue beam and hologram technologies in these 'last times' and in similar way, a 'Jesus' can appear when it is not truly Him coming yet, *Matthew 24, I Thessalonians 2*. We see this idea given through children's movies.

See Roger Spurr on YouTube[3] or Facebook,[4] who proves this in very simple scientific ways, full of common sense, aiding us to go out and look at rocks,

---

[3] https://www.youtube.com/channel/UC8v44qrU_Fdd7UN_XlUMpew
[4] https://www.facebook.com/roger.spurr.7

seeing this to be true. I myself found rocks of three different sizes, all with a red artery hole in the middle of each.

Health system including dentistry and optometry have methods to keep us buying into these systems, like teeth cleaning, braces, eyeglasses, checkups, increasing number of tests even for newborns, multiple vaccines, medicines, and diagnosis based on testing and protocol diagnosis. But the person tested is not sent to eat nutritionally first, then retested, in most cases. When there is a tiny dot-size cavity in a tooth, a large hole is drilled already damaging that strong tooth made by God. Teeth are placed in the gums with such strength!

True good 'natural' nutrition and common sense as God designed, are the best vitamins and minerals, plus an inner freeing through Him, appropriate home-based hygiene, some resonant sunshine, a bit of exercise (*I Timothy 4:8*) result in GOOD health that includes teeth, gums, bones, skin.

Even now with c-virus issue (2020), we observe that natural health methods are not being encouraged, instead Western medicine methods and chemicals are. Keep in mind that 'foods' like shrimp, lobster, catfish, pork have been commercialized to us as 'expensive' when all of these are cleaners of their surroundings.

We have lost ability to use plants and trees grown in nature as needed, to promote true health. My 5-year-old granddaughter already believes that 'the health care system' cures. God Himself cures as shown by Jesus, *II Chronicles 16:12. Daniel 1* explains how to get healthy and robust: eating natural foods, while honoring Him. Artificial chemicals do not heal (*dissonant*), and most disease situations are a temporary disorder in entire body due to ingesting processed foods. Satan can attack our health yet under God's guiding Hand, although difficult, yet His good can be achieved, *Job*.

Climate change has many causes: destruction of creation by commercial deforestation, destructive mining practices, climate-engineering, chemical trails done by non-passenger planes, rain manipulation, genetically modified crops, water treatment plants, chemicals in air conditioning systems, trash, and more.

Aliens (*Revelation 12:9, Revelation 9:1-12)* will have its time but are fallen angels working with Satan.

We are void of a literal, **comprehensive study of the complete Bible**, yet I think God does not allow this to be developed, because He allows Satan to think that he is 'winning', *I Corinthian 2:6-8, Revelation 7:9*. If we did such studies, it would allow us to understand the basis of the 'shadow' described in the 'old' covenant books that points to the Messiah in the 'new testament' books, where there is a testator, Who is the Messiah, *Hebrews*. This type of study gives much depth to our faith in God. Getting His Truth requires lots of time and study, *Proverbs 2*, because He is God and is the Source of All, including All thoughts from whence All is.

Jesus taught how to UNDERSTAND the heart use of the laws given (*Sower parable*), plus He heals in and out, full of God-compassion in spite of us being enemies with Him, *Romans 5:10-11*. Thereby we joy in God the Father through Jesus Christ, by whom we have now received the atonement.☺

We passively have received partial TRUTHS through cartoons, movies, commercials, video games, porn, churches, and books. The coming metaverse will be unlimited in such as a virtual non-physical world ☹ pointing to the opposite of God's ways, *James 3*.

Government care versus His Care; Israelites wanted a king instead.

Judicial system 'interprets' law, influenced by the very ones who rule the 'agendas' and it is said that they put in presidents. Money at present is petrodollar but that is changing right now very fast in 2022.

Permissions from government are needed for all steps of our life: birth to death, yet they have no control over our soul, its final destiny nor over our thoughts directly. They can only predict our thoughts by our behavior through social data collected, processed by AI computers.

Debt pressure is huge as all are encouraged to acquire mortgages to buy houses and other such (through credit). We are burdened by property taxes, HOA payments, car insurance as if we were buying a car, plus medical insurance. Just the sum of those is an income.☹ We make it worse through our own credit card buying.☹ Our true happiness is not in money and things but instead in each other and in our God, *Matthew 22:37-40, I Timothy 6:6-8*.

Crisis actors and false flags and disease scares are set-up to scare citizens to submit to government control. In a movie called *Wag the Dog* 1997, a movie director was hired to make a commercial that fooled the public, so the USA could go to war, then that producer was killed.

Wars are begun most times by combinations of world leaders desiring to gain access and control over natural resources, *Ezekiel 29:4, 38:4* 'hook in the jaw'.

Lives are lost in this deeply wrong greedy plan, plus the soldiers are trained to do cruel things and not 'feel' it. We are all mindlessly part of the 'beast' system, *Revelation 13*, through our very OWN opinions without studying the Biblical Truth, *Proverbs 1-3*. We cooperate with the divisive thesis/anti-thesis (*Jesuit*) Hegelian indoctrination about racism and/or skin color, cultures, national patriotism, religions, religious variations, political parties, etc. Yet we still 'trust' governments.

Character of God	Character of the Law
• JUST - Roman 3:26	• JUST - Roman 7:2
• TRUE - John 3:33	• TRUE - Neh 9:13
• PURE - I John 3:3	• PURE - Ps 19:7-8
• LIGHT - I John 1:5	• LIGHT - Prov 6:23
• FAITHFUL - I Cor 1:9	• FAITHFUL - Ps 118:86
• GOOD - Nahum 1:7	• GOOD - Rom 12:7, 16
• SPIRITUAL - I Cor 10:1-4	• SPIRITUAL - Rom 7:14
• HOLY - Is 6:3; I Pet 1:15	• HOLY - Ex 20:8; Rom 7:12
• TRUTH - John 14:6	• TRUTH - Ps 119:142, 151
• LIFE - I John 14:6	• LIFE - John 12:50; Mt 19:17
• RIGHTEOUSNESS - Jer 23:6	• RIGHTEOUSNESS - Ps 119:172
• PERFECT - Mt 5:48; Heb 13:8	• PERFECT - Ps 19:7; James 1:25
• FOREVER - John 8:35; Heb 13:8	• FOREVER - Ps 111:8; Luke 16:17

6

COVID – Return to USA

In December 2019, I visited the USA as usual, to celebrate holidays with my family, and precisely on the very day I was to return to my home, out of country, my mom passed. I was so glad that I was with her; additionally, she passed pleasantly, even with laughter. ☺ She needed to rest from her bodily difficulties and in that I was glad.

Prior to that moment, I had attempted to change my return ticket date in January 2020, because I had been sick but to no avail as they strangely repeated that I could not get a new date until August 2020. We had a wonderful family funeral time, in which my mom was described as a true inspirer and my cousins from Colorado sang. So, I decided to go visit my daughter again in West Texas before returning home and also my son and his wife, in the Dallas area.

I bought a new return ticket, but COVID hit, and airports were closed for months everywhere, people stranded world-wide.☹

In my case, I was 'stranded' where my family lives, buying a car during that time with my mom's inheritance. I mostly stayed with my daughter and her family, when in the middle of that year, 2020, she suffered a huge change, yet I was with her and her daughter. I am very thankful because my staying has aided them emotionally and to this day.

So, in September 2020, I bought yet another new ticket to travel home, just for two weeks and then return to USA to continue to aid my daughter. All was set for the trip including the COVID testing, when a very heavy object fell square on the top of one of my feet the day before I would travel. I could not walk for two days. I could not travel.

That same ticket was changed four times with no extra cost and finally fully refunded, but before that, I had a new date to travel in October 2020. I was in West Texas when a freak ice storm in October prevented me from travelling to DFW for the flight home, so I changed dates again, but that week, a 45-year-old cousin and his family got a very serious case of COVID that he continually published about on Facebook, stopping me in my tracks. So, I thought, "You, dear God Almighty, are encouraging me to NOT travel, right?"

My youngest son was especially pleased that I did not travel and to this day, he says I should not, not yet. Ticket was refunded a couple of months later and I live with my daughter and granddaughter.

Amazingly this stay allowed me to aid with the caring of my dad with my brothers until he passed in 2021, me being with him when he passed, which I am thankful. Then following that good family funeral time, soon after, my dad's oldest brother passed in Colorado, so I had the opportunity to go be with that family, when I had not been up there for 28 years.☺

Susan 'sandwich' story benefitted my daughter tremendously! One specific event in 2020, caused my daughter's heart to plunge to depths, but God Almighty already had a 'very enthusiastic Susan' ready to bless with her own story, with a daughter similar age with my granddaughter. My daughter and her met in a park close by just at the 'right' time and immediately Susan -super enthusiastic- from her own unusual life experiences, brought my daughter UP out of that extremely disappointing hole. Also, very soon afterwards, another friend "Susan" flew to our newer home from Florida, to do a week internet motivational conference with my daughter!

I call this God's "Susan Sandwich" for my daughter. Also in that same time frame, Susan with her young daughter, Katy, had already met Raquel with her small daughter, Mia, at that same park, so they became a threesome with their daughters; so fun! God at work in details over EACH person, yea!

Now, my daughter and I, both as believers in Jesus' desiring to learn to live in His wise ways, have learned to submit gladly to each other and have good dispositions with each other which is totally amazing as we are very opposite in much. It is wonderful, as I told her recently:

'you never imagined living with your mom again, huh?'

And for myself, a cat for me here in US so **'The Cat Story'**- my God-Given cat.☺ When we were already living in our apartment, the next year, 2021, a tiny kitten came walking into our yard, not afraid of the small dog nor of the adults in the back yard at that moment, so I called him Fearless. My granddaughter called him, Snoopy.

So Snoopy the Fearless, an outside cat, would sit in my lap often as a babe, because I loved being outside and love cats, plus he is a very affectionate cat.

Soon after, I travelled north to visit my youngest son and his fiancée for a month. When I returned, Snoopy was no longer around. About three and a half months later, we returned at night from a long trip and there he was at the back door, wow! He still sits in my lap when I am outside and follows me as I walk outside, which is unusual, indeed a God-given pet.

Cristina story: With a neighbor across the way, we would wave our hands to each other to say 'hi', but one day she came over for us to meet and asked me what books I read.

Truly in recent times, I would use YouTube more than reading books, but I could mention a few. She said that maybe we could exchange books to read. Later, I realized that one of my very favorite authors is John Piper, a very deep thinker. Plus, he wrote a book called *Desiring God*, so I thought, "I will go buy that book to share with her." Turns out that at the bookstore, I remembered several great authors like Watchman Nee, Max Lucado, and others.

So, I bought her that book but then I saw Piper's book called *When We do NOT Desire God*, and I bought that for me, plus a book by Watchman Nee called *A Life that Wins*, also for myself.

I bought for her and for me the book by John Bunyan *Pilgrim's Progress Part 1&2*, delightful allegorical reading about coming to Jesus and our walk through this temporary life. Through her initiative, I was very blessed to consider the following much better, pointing myself towards Jesus in this way: *II Chronicles 29:31*.

The congregation brought in sacrifices & thanksgiving offerings, **free heart** (burnt) offerings. *Deuteronomy 28:47-48*.

Because you serve not your God with joyfulness, gladness of heart for the abundance of all things, therefore you will serve your enemies, *Proverbs 14:12*. *Philippians 4:4* Rejoice in Jesus always; again, I say, Rejoice ☺ I am thankful!

End of discourse ☺

To go from an emotionally driven life to a life with wiser choices through our Savior is a lifetime experience.☺

John 13:34 Jesus Savior said: 'A new commandment I give to you, that you love one another as I have loved you' (gave His Life & Blood for us, like Passover).

> ***Ecclesiastes 12:1 Remember now thy Creator in the days of thy youth, while the evil days come not, nor the years draw nigh, when thou shalt say, I have no pleasure in them;*** [13-14] ***Let us hear the conclusion of the whole matter:***

- ❖ Fear God our Creator and Redeemer (*Isaiah*) and keep His Wisdom (*I Corinthians 1-2, Proverbs*), for this is the whole duty of man.

- ❖ For God shall bring every work into judgment, with every secret thing, whether it be good, or whether it be evil

- ❖ Physical death for believer in Jesus: *Luke 16:22*

- ❖ Angels take us. *II Corinthians 5:6-8* with Jesus. Jesus said to one on the cross next to Him that he would be with Him in Paradise

- ❖ We are conscious, *Luke 16:19-31*

- ❖ Are aware of past earth happenings, *Revelation 6:9-10*

- ❖ Will recognize people there, *Luke 16:24*.

- ❖ He is Alive and Coming ☺

- ❖ Then there will be the New Earth and New Heavens and New Jerusalem, all New.

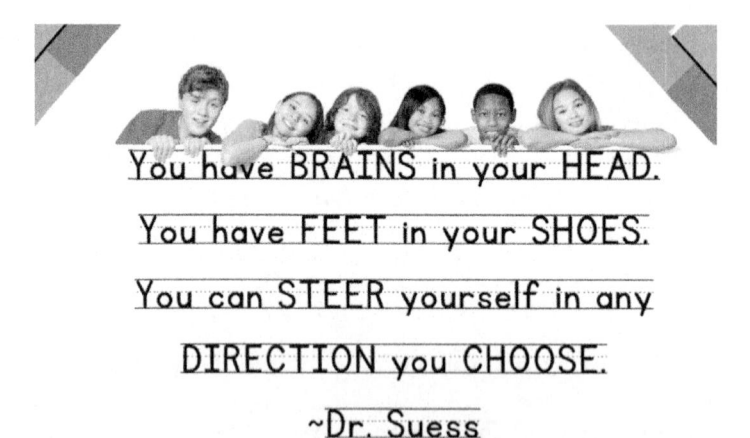

You have BRAINS in your HEAD.
You have FEET in your SHOES.
You can STEER yourself in any DIRECTION you CHOOSE.
~Dr. Suess

Appendices

A – WHO IS JESUS

Who is Jesus, according to my studies? **Bible was** written by many authors of different professions, ages & cultures speaking one Truth, that The Creator (*Genesis 1, John 1, Colossians 1, Hebrews 1*) made ALL (plus how He made All is explained, *Proverbs 8)*, giving angels and humans freedom to choose Him or not. Before the foundation of the creation, He had His Wise plan to save the unrighteous humans (*not the angels*) who are willing to go through HIS WAY, *Romans 10, I Corinthians 2:8*, through His Son, Jesus the Righteous, The Lamb of God.

The Old Testament or Covenants is the 'shadow'; the New Testament, the fulfilling of it, *Hebrews,* with a testator. Jesus said, 'this cup is the **new** testament in My blood, which is shed for you'*, Luke 22:20*. He is the First and the Last, *Isaiah 41:4, 43:13, 44:6, 48:12; Revelation 1:17, 2:8, 22:13*. In the English KJV, "I am He' is found in *John 4:26, Isaiah 41:4, 43:13, 48:12*. Prophecies are found in OT, like *Zechariah 12:10, Psalms 22, Isaiah 11* that point to Whom we call our Savior. Is Bible THE absolute truth?

Hebrews 10 explains that the law is the shadow of the OT which is fulfilled by Jesus as explained in the NT, *Colossians 2:16-17*. There are many witnesses about Jesus being the Son of the Father in Heaven: *John 1, John 3* (*Nicodemus*), *I John 1*, demons, centurion at the cross, Elizabeth's babe in womb (*John the Baptist*). Empires before and after Jesus till now, are same ones, *Revelation 17*. Archaeology affirms Bible in many instances.

Isaiah 2:2,4,11,17, And it shall come to pass in the last days, that the mountain of our God's house shall be established in the top of the mountains and shall be exalted above the hills; and all nations shall flow unto it. They shall beat their swords into plowshares, and their spears into pruning hooks: nation shall not lift up sword against nation; neither shall they learn war anymore. And God/Creator/Savior alone shall be exalted in that day. And the idols He shall utterly abolish.

Isaiah 9:2, 6-7 The people that walked in darkness have seen a great light. For unto us a child is born, a son is given; the government shall be upon His shoulder. His Name shall be called Wonderful Counsellor, The mighty God, The everlasting Father, The Prince of Peace.

Of the increase of His government and peace there shall be no end, upon the throne of David, to establish it with judgment, with justice from henceforth even forever. The zeal of the GOD of hosts will perform this.

Isaiah 11:1, Jeremiah 23:5-6 Branch out of Jesse's roots (David, Jesus).

Isaiah 25:8-10 He will swallow up death in victory; God will wipe away tears (*Revelation 7, 21*).And it shall be said in that day, 'Lo, this is our God; we have waited for Him, and He will save us. This is He; we will be glad and rejoice in His Salvation (*Romans 10*)'.For in this mountain shall the hand of our God/Creator/Savior rest.

Isaiah 53 crushed for us.

B -TIMELINE

Timeline is 6000 years from the creation to the announced Millennium period, years summed according to information given throughout Bible in total 7000 years then the White Throne and New Jerusalem where ALL is made New, *Revelation 21*.

We in Him are made new as first part of this wonderness. This timeline is akin to the creation timeline consisting of seven 24-hour days, *Exodus 20:11*, the seventh day for rest, *Hebrews 3-4* where Jesus is our Rest when we truly believe in Him. From the creation to Jesus' arising from the dead, are exactly 4000 years as calculated by Joseph Merrari and also confirmed by myself (see Hebreas in Facebook, video "Passage through the veil of time").[5]

The c-virus issue has awoken us more, yet we can too easily return to our 'comfort', eyes not on Jesus, THE CREATOR/OUR SAVIOUR. Some have explained that probably, the c-virus and its most recommended remedy are indeed the Seal 1 being opened by the Lamb, *John 1:29*, because of Greek root word for 'bow' is 'toxon.'

---

[5] https://www.facebook.com/watch/?v=1417712928333773&ref=sharing

Seal 2 could be qualified as Russia's aggression, combined with China, *Daniel 7:5*, which includes the monetary change from the petrodollar towards a world currency that influences Seal 3 where the money we gain in one day will suffice only for the daily food.

The *chapters 2:14, 8, 11 and 12 in Daniel* refer to the end times, just as each chapter of the book of *I Thessalonians* refers to HIS COMING.☺But *chapter 11* especially explains that God has 'appointed times' for the end (*Matthew 24:14*) just like *Revelation 9:15*.

Seal 4 is called DEATH, over ¼ of the earth. *Revelation 17-18* describes Mystery Babylon that overrides this.

Before the Trumpets, there will be a huge earthquake, Seal 6 but is not the biggest one is described in *Revelation 16*.

The Final 'Tower of Babel' Reset: World Economic Forum has clearly stated in 2022 that there is a structured, systematic 2022-2023 reset going on, where our normal supply chain is being changed, going towards eliminating our natural foods like meat in which laboratory-made foods will be the new way. They plan that AI algorithm-data will drive all, perhaps then related to the 'mark of the beast system'.

A basic salary is said to be given to those people who cooperate fully with new world order, *Revelation 13:17, 14:9*.

In 2024, a second solar eclipse will occur in April, marking an 'x' over the USA when combined with the map of 2017 solar eclipse, plus the USA will have the presidential elections.

Deagel defense page shows that especially several main NATO countries will have lost 2/3 population each by 2025, including the USA.

The ones pushing for global governance have said that the neuro-brain link will be ready in 2026, *Revelation 13* for 42 months: *Daniel 9:27, 11:31,12:11, Matthew 24:14-15* gospel to the world through persecution, then end comes with the appearance of the abomination that causes desolation. Then, *Jude 14, Revelation 19, 1 Thessalonians 4:14* bring us with Him.

C - TRUE ASTRONOMY

True Astronomy

Genesis 1:9 gather 'waters below' and 'dry land' appeared on Day 3 and was planted (*Genesis 2:5-6*), called Earth. God sits over the circle of the earth, *Isaiah 40*. *Isaiah 66:1* Earth is My footstool.

Sun, moon and stars are a light (see *Genesis 1:14-18, I Corinthians 15, Revelation 1:20*). The Sun is NOT a star as is taught in astronomy nor does the moon reflect sunlight.

Revelation 1 says that all eyes will see Jesus when He comes. The devil took Jesus to a very high mountain to see ALL the WORLD empires, *Matthew 4:8*.

Harry Katz[6], YouTube, explains how The Tabernacle that Moses built according to the pattern shown to him by God (*Exodus 25:49.40; Hebrews 8:5*) infers the following: **Holy of Holiest** = His Throne in Heaven.

Sanctuary with Bread and Candle Holders is the space between Throne and land or Earth (not measurable, *Jeremiah 31:37*).

---

[6]https://www.youtube.com/channel/UCtsvvToQDUzaJMrUyHN5M_w

All of this also implies that the **Laver** is oceans with land, the **Burnt offering altar** is Hades, and the "Milky Way" are the **'hooks'** between the stretched curtains as a tent, *Exodus 38, Isaiah 40, Psalms 104:2.*

In August 2017, a solar eclipse occurred in USA, where the darkest portion of the shadow across was only 70 miles wide. So, if the moon was covering the sun as we are taught, with a diameter of over 2000 miles, that does not produce a dark neat shadow of only 70 miles. I took a tennis ball with a light source over it to verify the idea of the size of its shadow at its neatest darkness shadow. As I moved the light source around, there was a distance where the shadow was the darkest and not diffuse and it was the same size as the tennis ball. I also took pictures of that solar eclipse in 2017 and used other pictures that people published, inverting the colors. It was easy to observe that no round object was causing the indention in the Sun. Many conclude that the Sun eclipses and Moon phases are electric instead. In 2024, it is said that the USA will experience yet another such eclipse making an 'X' over the USA. I will definitely be driving to see this in Texas and take further pictures.

Psalms 19:4-6, God set a tabernacle for the Sun, which is as a bridegroom coming out of his chamber, *Joel 2:16,* and rejoices as a strong man to run a race.

His going forth is from the end of the heaven and its circuit <u>unto the ends of it</u>; there is <u>nothing hid from its heat thereof.</u>

This reading infers that only our Sun heats all and covers what is true space.

Mark 13:24 in those days, after that tribulation, the sun shall be darkened, and **the moon shall not give her light**, *Ezekiel 32:7, Isaiah 13:10.*

Joshua 10:13 Sun came to be still and moon too.

MY FINAL THOUGHTS

As I leave you with these thoughts in my book, I feel so privileged to share His Steps in my life with you who took time to read my nerdy thoughts, and strongly encourage you to do the same. Contact me as you need: mn5db5@yahoo.com ☺ I urge you to reread this book looking verse up. ☺

Please, if you have not formally said 'YES' to Jesus who is Creator, *John 1, Colossians 1, Hebrews 1* (look this up) and Savior, look up *Isaiah 43:11, Hosea 13:4, Isaiah 53, and 1 Timothy 3:16.*

I aid you in a prayer here (feel free to say it as you need to): key is *Romans 10.* Believe in your heart in Him, His Righteousness and that His Blood cleanses us from sin, saying this with your mouth.

Dear Jesus,

Please forgive me for all my sins. I recognize I cannot live in this world without you. Please deliver, heal and set me free. Help me to forgive those that have hurt me. Come into my heart and show me who You are. I give you all of me. I want to honor you with my life and the rest of my destiny here on Earth. Use me for your glory. In Jesus name. Amen.

Printed in Great Britain
by Amazon